RISE OF THE ENEMY

A Dragon Slayer Bible Story

Book Zero

Laurie Christine

SWEET BAY
MEDIA

ENDORSEMENTS FOR THE DRAGON SLAYER BIBLE SERIES

Laurie understands that boys hunger for adventure and desire to be counted among the heroic. God made them that way. My two sons, both voracious readers and now grown, would have loved this adventurous challenge to godly living!

MARK HANCOCK, CEO of Trail Life USA

Laurie has a heart for boys and their parents. She invites boys into adventure and purpose, two things they crave throughout development.

DAVID THOMAS, Cohost of Raising Boys and Girls podcast; author of *Wild Things: The Art of Nurturing Boys* and *Raising Emotionally Strong Boys*

I highly recommend this series for parents, grandparents, Sunday School teachers, and children's ministry workers who want to engage their children with the Bible in a creative and imaginative way. Laurie Christine depicts Jesus as the "Dragon Slayer" and Satan as a physical dragon to help young readers connect with biblical truths and use their spiritual strength to conquer the enemies of their lives.

DR. SCOTT TURANSKY, Cofounder of the National Center for Biblical Parenting, Author of *Parenting is Heart Work*

Angels and demons. Dragons and Dragon Slayers. Your boys are going to love this series. This series will not only hold the attention of boys, it will inspire and equip them to identify the schemes of the devil and resist his evil plan.

TIM SHOEMAKER, Author of High Water Series and *The Very Best, Hands-On, Kinda Dangerous Family Devotions*

The level of spiritual battle surrounding youth today calls parents to prepare their children with thoughtful, biblically-grounded learning and conversations. Laurie Christine has created an engaging, encouraging resource to equip kids with vital truths about their spiritual enemy and the power they have in Christ.

LYNNE JACKSON, Cofounder of Connected Families

In a culture where wrong is right and right is wrong, where biblical truth is not only questioned but maligned at every turn, followers of Jesus must be bold and courageous in their quest to stand firm in truth while simultaneously sharing the love and light of the Gospel. This quest is not just for adults. The dragon is out for the souls of our kids too.

In The Dragon Slayer Bible Series, Laurie inspires preteen readers to join the army of the King of kings, to live courageously in his power, and to experience the victory they can have over the enemy as they trust in him.

**KATHY NOEL, Director of Child Discipleship,
Calvary Church, Lancaster, PA**

Every boy longs to be part of an epic adventure. The Dragon Slayer Bible Series is the ideal fusion of story and practical insights to invite young men to take a stand with God—for good!

ALLEN ARNOLD, Wild at Heart Ministries

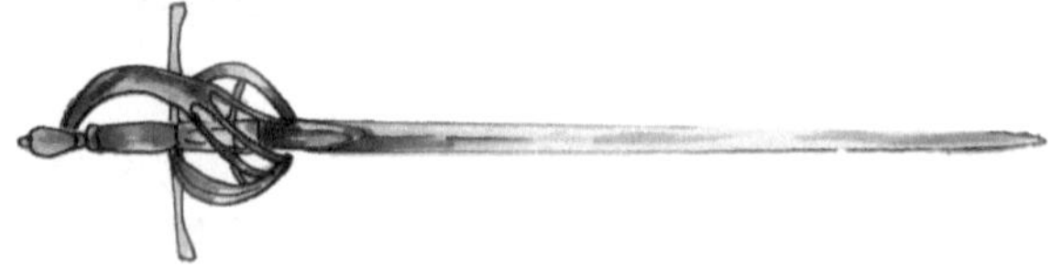

FOR MY COURAGEOUS BOYS

Elliott, Oliver, Thatcher, and Pierson

Be strong and courageous! Do not be afraid or discouraged. For the Lord your God is with you wherever you go.

Joshua 1:9

CONTENTS

REVELATION 12:7-9

Then there was war in heaven. Michael and his angels fought against the dragon and his angels. And the dragon lost the battle, and he and his angels were forced out of heaven. This great dragon—the ancient serpent called the devil, or Satan, the one deceiving the whole world—was thrown down to the earth with all his angels.

COURAGEOUS WARRIORS NEEDED

Will you join the armies of the Dragon Slayer? Grab your sword and fight the evil dragon. Your life depends on it. Your quest, should you choose to accept it, will be long and difficult. You will face dangers and enemies along the way. But don't lose heart. The Dragon Slayer will equip you with the weapons you need and the strength to keep going. He will fight alongside you!

And in the end, you will hear Him declare, "Well done, courageous warrior."

ABOUT THE BOOK

Rise of the Enemy is "Book Zero" in the Dragon Slayer Bible Series. It's a prequel to the main books in the series. (*Rise of the Enemy* was originally published as Book 1 in the series. If you own a copy that says "Book One", congratulations! You have a rare limited edition!)

Book one in the series is *Garden of Mysteries: A Dragon Slayer Bible Story*, along with its companion devotional *Garden of Mysteries: A Dragon Slayer Devotional*.

Rise of the Enemy is part action-packed biblical fiction, part devotional, and part Bible study. The book is divided into three sections: *The Message*, *The Mission*, and *The Marching Orders*. Read the book front to back. Below is a description of each section:

The Message

This part contains an adventure-packed fictional narrative based on a Bible story. My desire is for you to experience the thoughts and emotions of the main biblical characters in the story while gaining a clearer picture of our glorious God.

Have You Joined the Army? explains God's plan of salvation.

The Mission

This part is a call to action that reads like a devotional. The archangel Michael invites readers to join the army of the Dragon Slayer. He explains *The Message* part of the book and encourages readers to fight courageously in the battle against the evil dragon.

The Marching Orders

This section contains five daily devotional readings for you to complete one day at a time.

Basic Training provides Bible passages for you to read.

Directives dives into the Scripture passage and challenges you to understand and live out the Word of God.

Critical Communications is a prayer to the God of Angel Armies.

Battle Plan provides you with space to think and reflect on the challenge for the day.

The Extra Stuff

Small Group Discussion Questions can be downloaded at www.LaurieChristine.com/dragon-slayer-bible/discussion-guides

Did You Know? provides interesting facts about the story.

Background Scriptures provides additional Scripture passages that support the story.

Glossary defines terms used in the story that may be unfamiliar.

More About the Book

Rise of the Enemy, A Dragon Slayer Bible Story, has been checked for theological accuracy by Gordon Gregory, ThD. Dr. Gregory received his Master's of Theology degree from Dallas Theological Seminary and his Doctorate of Theology from the University of South Africa. He currently serves as Professor of Bible and Theology at Lancaster Bible College and Capital Seminary & Graduate School.

This book remains true to what the Bible reveals about God's character, and what the Bible teaches about spiritual warfare. Jesus is referred to as the Dragon Slayer, and Satan is depicted as a dragon. The Bible uses a lot of dragon and serpent imagery when talking about Satan (Revelation 12).

The goal of this book is three-fold:

1. To provide an entertaining experience for the reader in the context of biblical history.

2. To challenge the reader to dig deeper into the Scriptures and to learn about the characters and events mentioned in the story.

3. To make readers aware that we have an evil enemy who seeks to destroy us.

My prayer is that this book will inspire young readers to dig deeper into God's Word and put their trust in the Dragon Slayer!

THE MESSAGE

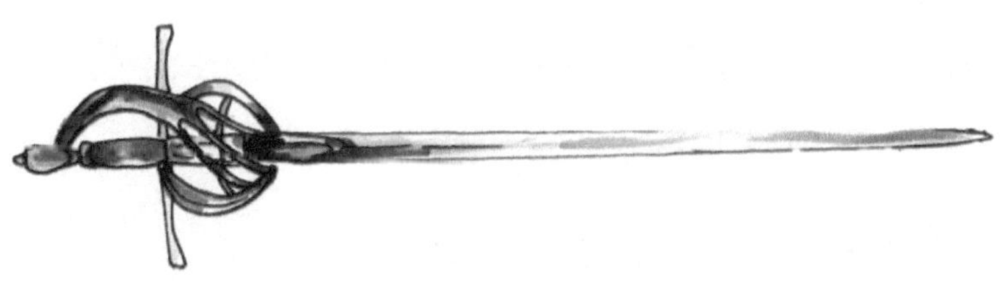

THE REBELLION

THE MESSAGE: PART 1

Have you heard about the war in Heaven?

My name is Michael. I am captain of the angel armies. Long ago, we angels lived in Heaven—thousands of us—all created to serve and worship the King.

But the most beautiful angel, Lucifer, decided he wanted more power than the King.

I remember the day the war started.

Midway through my daily report to the King, the door of the throne room burst open.

Lucifer stormed in. His hair shone like a thousand diamonds. A rainbow of gems adorned the hem of his robe. As he strode across the room, light from the throne reflected off the gems, creating a magnificent kaleidoscope on the marble floor.

Our eyes met, and the corner of his mouth curled into a sneer. He lifted his chin and tossed his head, flinging his long, sparkling hair over one shoulder.

Lucifer and I used to be friends, but we no longer had much in common. Not since he became obsessed with his own beauty and the power the King gave him.

He shoved past me and marched to the throne.

Was he crazy? The King allowed no one to approach him without permission.

Lucifer grabbed the hilt of his sword, yanked it from its sheath, and raised it over his head. The sleeve of his robe slid up to his shoulder, revealing his muscled bicep. Powerful wings unfurled behind him and quivered with anticipation.

I glanced up at the King. His eyes narrowed. This would not end well for Lucifer.

"I've had enough!" Lucifer bellowed, staring the King in the eyes. "Everyone can see I'm more beautiful and more powerful than all the other angels." He cast a sideways glance in my direction. "I deserve more."

My hand slipped to the hilt of my sword and I tightened my fist. What was he saying? The King had given him so much. Did he have no respect?

Lucifer stepped toward the throne, brandishing his sword in front of him. "I don't need to submit to this king." He thrust his finger toward the throne. "Who put him in charge, anyway?"

The King's eyes flashed with a fire I had never seen before. A chill ran up my spine.

"Silence!" The King's voice bounced off the walls of the throne room. "Are you defying me? I AM the only King. I AM the only one worthy of worship. How dare you plot against me!"

Lucifer's face contorted with rage as he raised both hands above his head. "Armies of the dragon—unite!"

The roar of his voice shook the entire palace. I spread my arms to steady myself.

Who was this dragon? We were about to find out.

The Traitor

The Message: Part 2

A swarm of angels flew in through the windows and door, swords drawn. They formed a half-circle around Lucifer, all facing the throne.

What was going on? Were these angels on Lucifer's side? Did they think they could overthrow the King of Heaven?

Not if I could help it.

I drew my sword, and heat filled my chest. No matter the cost, I would fight for my King. I looked to the throne, waiting for orders.

The King nodded slightly.

I knew what I had to do.

"Loyal armies of the King," I shouted.

Immediately, a second host of angels from all corners of the kingdom arrived.

"We have a traitor in our ranks! It's time to fight!"

The swoosh of wings and the clash of swords sounded throughout the palace. Angels fighting against angels—was this really happening?

Across the room, Lucifer shoved through the throng of heavenly beings toward the King. I spread my wings and flew after him. I landed in front of him, and our swords met in midair with a mighty clang.

Sweat dripped down my arms. I raised my sword over my head, gripping it with two hands. I gritted my teeth, ready to crush the head of the enemy.

Crack!

But it wasn't the crack of Lucifer's head. As I was about to bring the final blow, a loud crash split the air. Bright light and black smoke filled the throne room.

An enormous dragon crouched in the place where Lucifer had stood. Its scales glinted like flames of fire, and powerful wings unfurled to twice the length of its body.

I ducked and jumped away to keep from getting knocked down by one of the wings.

Sharp spikes barbed the dragon's back. Its tail swept back and forth across the floor of the palace, threatening to wipe out anyone in its way. Tendrils of smoke seeped out of the dragon's nose as its beady black eyes stared back at me.

What. Just. Happened? Lucifer is … a dragon?

The King rose to his feet, and the entire battle scene froze. Silence fell over the room.

The King glared at the dragon. "Lucifer, you are no longer welcome here. You have defied me and have proven a traitor to my throne. You had more power than anyone in Heaven save myself. But you wanted more. For this act of treason, you and your followers shall never again have a place in my kingdom."

I shuddered. To be kicked out of Heaven was an unimaginable fate.

"You will never win, oh king." The dragon sneered. The voice was still Lucifer's, but it was deeper and gravelly with a slight hiss. "You may have defeated us today in this battle, but you have not seen the last of me!"

An icy numbness crept into my chest. This drag-on was pure evil. I knew I'd just witnessed an event that would forever change our future.

THE PLAN
THE MESSAGE: PART 3

The dragon squinted his beady eyes and swished his tail.

"But how to defeat you . . ." he muttered to himself.

I coughed, trying not to choke on the dragon's smoky breath.

"Ah! I know." Lucifer's charred lips formed a tight smile as another puff of smoke blew from his nostrils. He arched his back and leveled himself with the King's throne. "You know those people you just created—the ones you call your favorites?"

My stomach twisted. What was Lucifer scheming?

The King had recently created new beings called people. He put them in a magnificent garden on a place called Earth. No way the King would allow Lucifer anywhere near his new creation. *Would he?* The King loved these people like his own children and talked with them like his best friends. Lucifer had been jealous from the beginning.

The King tightened his fist around his scepter, his knuckles white. His jaw tightened and his eyes narrowed.

The dragon bobbed his scaly head as if daring the King to a duel. "Maybe I'll pay them a little visit." He threw back his head and laughed. "Ha! Then we'll see who is most powerful. We'll see who deserves to be worshipped."

"Lucifer, get out." Determination filled the King's eyes, but also sadness.

The dragon opened his wings. Thick, scaly skin stretched between each of the finger-like bones. He let out an ear-piercing screech, pushed off the floor in one powerful movement, and flew out of the palace. The angels who supported him, about one-third of Heaven's armies, took flight and followed their new master.

I stared in disbelief. Would Lucifer actually get away with this?

The King sighed and sat back down on his throne.

"My Lord, what would you like me to do?" I asked. "Should I go after them? Chase them down? Destroy them?" I was ready to fight these enemies to the death.

The King shook his head. "No, Michael. Let them go. This is not the last we will see of the dragon. You'll have plenty of chances to fight him. But don't worry. I have a plan to defeat him once and for all." A faint smile tugged at the corner of the King's mouth.

I let out a deep breath, thankful for the King's confidence after all that just happened.

"One day in the distant future, I will send my Son to make everything right again." The King's eyes brightened. "He will be called the Dragon Slayer, and he will destroy the evil beast."

A tingle ran up my arms, and my wings quivered at the mention of the King's Son. The Son was the Crown Prince—heir to the throne of Heaven.

And the Crown Prince would one day destroy the dragon?

Now this was a battle I did not want to miss.

Have You Joined the Army?

Courageous warrior, have you joined the army of the Dragon Slayer? Have you committed your life to serve him and fight for his Kingdom?

In the Garden of Eden, Adam and Eve chose to believe the dragon's lie instead of God's truth. As a result, their hearts were filled with an evil called sin. Every human since then has been born with the sickness of sin in their hearts.

Sin is not just the bad things you do or the ways you disobey God. Sin is buried deep in your heart. We can't measure up to God's perfect standard.

Romans 3:23 says, ***"For everyone has sinned; we all fall short of God's glorious standard."***

And the worst part is, our sin separates us from God and keeps us from having a close friendship with him. Our sin deserves to be punished, and that punishment is death—separation from God for eternity.

God loves you too much to remain separated from you forever. But in order for God to have a close friendship with you, the penalty for your sin must be paid.

Romans 6:23 says, *"The wages of sin is death."*

That's why God sent Jesus, the Dragon Slayer, his own perfect Son. When Jesus died on the cross, he took the punishment you deserved. When Jesus rose again from the dead, he gave you new life in him.

Romans 6:23 goes on to say, *"But the free gift of God is eternal life through Christ Jesus our Lord."*

God gives us life that will last forever! But how do you receive this gift of eternal life?

Ephesians 2:8-9 says, **"God saved you by his grace when you believed. And you can't take credit for this; it is a gift from God. Salvation is not a reward for the good things we have done, so none of us can boast about it."**

Did you catch it? God saved you when you *believed*. It's a free gift from God! All you need to do is believe in Jesus Christ.

John 3:16 says, **"For this is how God loved the world: He gave his one and only Son, so that everyone who believes in him will not perish but have eternal life."**

This is great news! Whoever believes in Jesus will not perish!

If you believe in Jesus and want him to be your Savior, try talking to God and saying something like this:

God of Angel Armies, I know my sin separates me from you. I know I can't measure up to your goodness. I believe that Jesus took the punishment I deserve when he died on the cross. I believe he gave me eternal life when he rose from the dead. I want you to be my Savior and Lord. I choose to join your army today and fight for your kingdom. Amen.

There is nothing magical about the words of this prayer. They are simply a guide to help you communicate with God. Jesus is the one who saves you.

When you believe in Jesus and trust him to be your Savior, you not only join God's army, but his family! The Bible says God is your Heavenly Father, and he loves you like his own child. You are now a son of the King of Heaven!

Now that you've joined the armies of the Drag-on Slayer, what's next?

God has given us many tools to help us fight the battle against the enemy. He has given us the Holy Spirit to help us and empower us. He has given us his Word, the Bible, to guide us. He has given us special armor to protect us.

Talk to an adult in your life who you respect and who has also believed in Jesus. It might be your mom or dad, a grandparent, a Sunday School teacher, a coach, or a pastor. Ask them to pray for you and encourage you as you learn what it means to be a child of God.

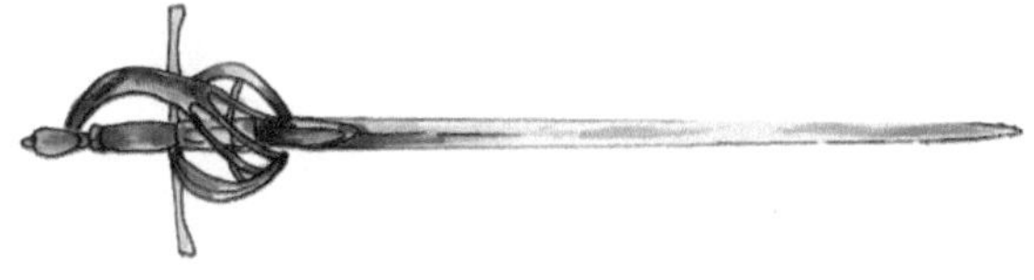

THE
MISSION

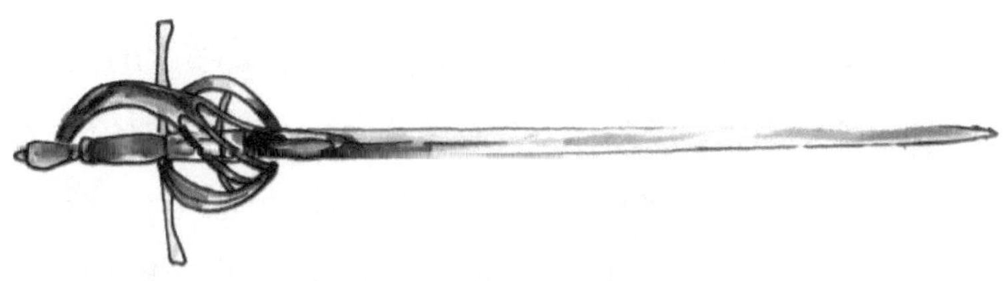

THE RESCUER

THE MISSION: PART 1

Greetings, courageous warrior!

We meet again. I am Michael, captain of the angel armies. On behalf of the Dragon Slayer, Son of the King of Heaven, I invite you to join me in an epic battle of good versus evil.

You read in *The Message* how the dragon, Lucifer, rebelled against the King and tried to overthrow the throne. He failed, and the King threw him out of Heaven, along with an army of fallen angels.

Lucifer has had many names and disguises over the years, including the devil, Satan, the Evil One, the serpent, and the dragon.

For thousands of years, the dragon has tried to destroy the beautiful people the King created.

His goal is to convince as many people as possible to join his armies and fight against the King.

But the King had a plan to defeat the dragon from the beginning of time. The King promised he would one day send a Rescuer to slay the dragon, destroy death, and restore the broken friendship between the King and his creation.

The King sent Jesus, his own Son, to fight the dragon and save his people.

But the battle didn't look like any human expected.

God's people were waiting for someone mighty and powerful to swoop in and save the day. But that's not how it happened.

When Jesus arrived on Earth, he came as a tiny human baby. He was helpless and poor, not a rich, powerful ruler. Everyone was shocked. Many didn't believe he could be the promised Rescuer.

But the King of Heaven often acts in mysterious ways.

THE BATTLE

THE MISSION: PART 2

You may wonder how Jesus fought the evil dragon if he was a helpless baby.

Well, he grew up to be a child, just like you. And then he grew up to be an adult, just like you'll be someday.

And then he died.

I know what you're thinking: "Wait, what? He died? I thought he was going to defeat the dragon! I thought there was going to be an epic battle!"

Well, there *was* an epic battle. Only no one could see it—at least no one on Earth.

Nobody saw the dragon swishing his tail or flicking his tongue as he eagerly awaited Jesus's birth. Nobody saw the dragon lurking behind every shrub and building when Jesus played in the streets of Nazareth as a child. Nobody saw the dragon trying to convince Jesus to worship him in the wilderness.

And nobody saw the dragon shrieking with delight when the Roman soldiers pounded spikes into Jesus's flesh, nailing him to a cross to die.

But what the dragon didn't know was that in the act of dying, Jesus destroyed him. In the very moment he thought he had triumphed, Jesus defeated him.

When Jesus died, he paid the punishment you deserved because of your sin. If you join the armies of the Dragon Slayer, the dragon can't accuse you. He can't taunt you and try to convince you that you are worth nothing.

Because to the King, you are worth everything. Jesus proved how much you are worth when he died for you.

The King loves you so much. That's why he sent Jesus to Earth in the first place. He hates that

the dragon brought evil into the world and ru-
ined your relationship with him. He loves you
too much to let your sin separate you from him
forever.

So when Jesus came to Earth, he solved the
problem of sin. Evil no longer controls you. You
are free from the sin that once held you captive.
The Dragon Slayer has defeated the dragon!

THE VICTORY
THE MISSION: PART 3

Do you know how the story ends? For three days, the dragon and his armies roared in victory, thinking they had won the war.

But the dragon had forgotten a prophecy from the beginning of time. It was a prophecy about Jesus, the Dragon Slayer, that the King had given to Adam and Eve in the Garden of Eden.

The prophecy said that one day the Dragon Slayer would come to Earth, and the dragon would attempt to destroy him—but he would fail. The dragon would merely injure Jesus, but then Jesus would crush the dragon.

For three days after Jesus was crucified, his body lay encased in a cold, dark tomb. But on Sunday morning, the dragon watched in horror as power from the throne of Heaven descended upon

Jesus. He cringed when he saw Jesus's lungs fill with air, his pale skin grow pink, and strength return to his lifeless bones. The dragon covered his head in terror when a burst of light exploded from the tomb and Jesus stood, raising his fists in triumph.

Jesus was alive again.

The dragon is defeated. Death no longer reigns. Sin has lost its power—even over you, my brave warrior.

But here's the deal. The dragon wants you to think he's still in charge. He is a liar and deceiver. And he's still trying to win the war.

That's why I invite you to join me in the King's battle against the evil dragon.

It's going to be tough. You will want to give up at times. But don't be afraid. Don't be discouraged. The King can help you to be strong and courageous. There might be setbacks. There will definitely be disappointments along the way.

But the Dragon Slayer promises never to leave your side. He's going with you into battle!

And do you know what else? He's going to give you special armor to wear that will protect you as you fight. The King designed it himself. You will learn about this armor a bit later.

For now, I need to know one thing. Are you with us? Will you pick up your sword and join me in fighting the dragon? Will you swear your allegiance to the Dragon Slayer and the armies of the King of Heaven?

THE MARCHING ORDERS

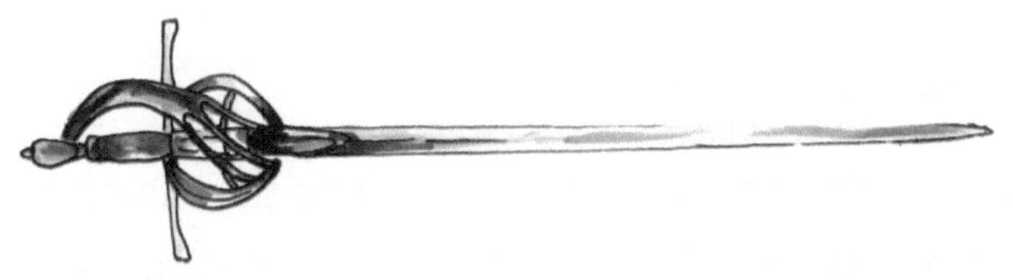

THERE IS ONLY ONE GOD

THE MARCHING ORDERS: DAY 1

BASIC TRAINING

Deuteronomy 4:39

[39] Remember this and keep it firmly in mind: The Lord is God both in heaven and on earth, and there is no other.

Nehemiah 9:6

[6] You alone are the Lord. You made the skies and the heavens and all the stars. You made the earth and the seas and everything in them. You preserve them all, and the angels of heaven worship you.

Isaiah 44:6-8

6 This is what the Lord says—Israel's King and Redeemer, the Lord of Heaven's Armies: "I am the First and the Last; there is no other God.

7 Who is like me? Let him step forward and prove to you his power. . . .

8 Is there any other God? No! There is no other Rock—not one!"

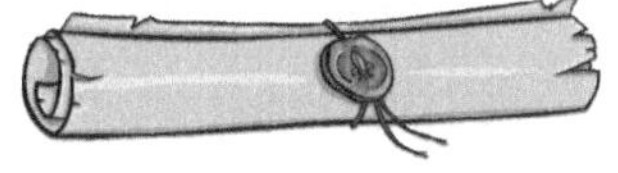

DIRECTIVES

Lucifer wanted to be like God. He thought he could become more powerful than God. But the Bible is clear that there is only one God. There is no other God besides the Lord.

In Isaiah 44:6-8, God asks, ***"Who is like me? Let him step forward and prove to you his power."***

God knows there is no other god or being as powerful as he is. He dares anyone to prove him wrong—which was exactly what Lucifer tried to do. As a result, the King kicked him out of Heaven.

God asks again, ***"Is there any other God?"*** And then he answers his own question: ***"No! There is no other Rock—not one!"***

Sometimes we think that we know better than God. We think we know what's best for our lives. We think: "Everything would be great, if only God would put *me* in charge." But we saw what happened when Lucifer tried to take control. He thought Heaven might be better if he was in charge. And then God kicked him out.

Throughout the Bible, God warned his people, the Israelites, to turn away from idols and stop worshipping false gods. The people didn't listen, and God had to punish them for their disobedience.

Even today, many nations and religions around the world worship gods other than the one true God. But Psalm 96:5 says, "The gods of other nations are mere idols, but the Lord made the heavens!"

The King who created the heavens also made you. He knows everything about you. He knows what makes you excited and what makes you afraid. He knows who your friends will be next year and whether or not you will make the football team.

He loves you more than anyone could ever love you, and he wants what's best for you.

Life doesn't work out for us when we try to put ourselves in God's place—when we think we would do a better job of being God than God himself.

CRITICAL COMMUNICATIONS

PRAY: King of Angel Armies, I know you are the only true God. You are the only one who deserves my worship. There is no one as powerful as you. I want you to be my God. I will serve no other God but you.

BATTLE PLAN

Think about a time when you thought you knew better than God. How did it work out? Use the space on the next page to write out your commitment to God to serve only him. Tell him you want him, and no one else, to be King of your life.

You Have an Enemy

The Marching Orders: Day 2

BASIC TRAINING

John 8:44

44 He [the devil] was a murderer from the beginning. He has always hated the truth, because there is no truth in him. When he lies, it is consistent with his character; for he is a liar and the father of lies.

I Peter 5:8-9a

8 Stay alert! Watch out for your great enemy, the devil. He prowls around like a roaring lion, looking for someone to devour.

9 Stand firm against him, and be strong in your faith.

I John 3:8

8 But when people keep on sinning, it shows that they belong to the devil, who has been sinning since the beginning. But the Son of God came to destroy the works of the devil.

DIRECTIVES

You have an enemy, young warrior. His goal is to destroy your life. He is a liar, a deceiver, and a murderer. He is known by many names including: the dragon, the Serpent, the devil, the Evil One, the deceiver, Lucifer, and Satan.

First Peter 5:8 describes him as a roaring lion prowling around, looking for someone to devour.

There is a whole world of invisible, spiritual creatures fighting a battle around us. The Dragon Slayer and his armies war against the dragon and his armies. The enemy strives to control your mind and heart. He wants you to turn away from the one true God. He wants you to reject the truth of God's Word, the Bible.

What should you do? Should you pee your pants and hide under your bed?

Look closely at what God commands us to do in I Peter 5:

Stay alert!

Watch out!

Stand firm!

Be strong!

What does it look like to be strong in your faith? Can you put your faith in anything you want?

Imagine this: If you have faith that you can walk across a pond on top of the water all on your own, do you think you could do it? Of course not! It doesn't matter how much faith you have if your faith is in the wrong thing.

Now imagine that the water is frozen solid, ten feet thick. Do you think you could walk across the lake? Sure you could!

What if you didn't have much faith? What if you were terrified that the ice would crack? Would the lake still hold you? You bet!

The *amount* of faith you had in the water doesn't matter compared to the *object* of your faith.

When God says, "Be strong in your faith," he's not talking about faith in your big muscles, or your good looks, or even your charming personality. Your faith must be in God—in Jesus—the only one who has the power to destroy the evil dragon.

CRITICAL COMMUNICATIONS

PRAY: God of Angel Armies, please help me stand firm against the attacks of the evil dragon. Help me be alert and aware of his schemes. Strengthen my faith in you! Don't let the lies of the enemy deceive me.

BATTLE PLAN

What have you been putting your faith in lately? Where have you been looking for your strength? Write out your answer on the next page. Then ask God to strengthen your faith in him and help you stand strong against the Evil One.

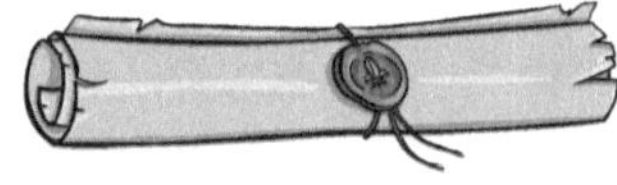

Be Strong in the Lord

The Marching Orders: Day 3

BASIC TRAINING

Ephesians 6:10-13

[10] A final word: Be strong in the Lord and in his mighty power.

[11] Put on all of God's armor so that you will be able to stand firm against all strategies of the devil.

[12] For we are not fighting against flesh-and-blood enemies, but against evil rulers and authorities of the unseen world, against mighty powers in this dark world, and against evil spirits in the heavenly places.

¹³ Therefore, put on every piece of God's armor so you will be able to resist the enemy in the time of evil. Then after the battle you will still be standing firm.

DIRECTIVES

In the last chapter, you learned that you have an enemy, the dragon, who wants to destroy you. You may have been thinking: "How am I supposed to fight a dragon when I can't see it? I don't even own a sword!"

Courageous warrior, there is no need to be afraid. God has given you everything you need to fight against the dragon. Let's take a closer look at the Bible passage from Ephesians 6.

There are a lot of things God tells us to do in order to fight the enemy. Grab a few colored pencils or highlighters for this part. Are you ready?

Read Ephesians 6:10-13 in your Basic Training. First, God commands us again to be strong. Take a colored pencil or highlighter and circle the words "Be strong." Every time we come across a command in this passage, we're going to circle it.

Look at what comes next: ***"Be strong . . . <u>in the Lord and in his mighty power."</u>***

Underline that last part! Does God want you to be strong by lifting weights? Nope! God wants you to be strong *in him* and in his strength.

Next, there's another command. Go back and circle the command in verse 11. We are commanded to ***"Put on all of God's armor."***

Why? God tells us to put on armor so that we will be able to stand firm against the devil's strategies to defeat us.

The next verse is pretty incredible. In the last chapter, we learned we are not fighting a physical battle we can see, but rather a spiritual battle we cannot see.

Read verse 12 again and underline what we are fighting against: ***evil spirits in the heavenly places.***

Sounds pretty intense! Aren't you glad God has provided you with the armor you'll need to withstand the enemy's attacks?

Verse 13 repeats the command to put on all of God's armor so that you will be able to resist the enemy. In the next chapter, we'll take a look at each piece of armor that God has provided for you.

But why do you need to put on all this armor? Because it's wartime! It's time for action. You can't just sit around on your caboose and expect to win any battles. It's time to grab your sword and join the armies of the Dragon Slayer. Are you in?

CRITICAL COMMUNICATIONS

PRAY: God of Angel Armies, sometimes I'm tempted to fight battles in my own strength. Other days I'm tempted to give in and not fight at all. Help me remember that my strength comes from you. Give me the power to put on the armor you have given me. I want to stand firm against any strategies the dragon may use against me. I am trusting in the Dragon Slayer and his mighty power.

BATTLE PLAN

Imagine yourself fighting in a spiritual battle. What sorts of things do you think the enemy might tempt you to do? What lies might he tell you in an attempt to win your heart? Use the half of the chart on the next page to write out one of the dragon's lies. Then, on the other half, write out God's truth for that same situation.

For example:

The Dragon's Lie: It's okay to hit my brother when I get angry.

God's Truth: God can help me be patient and show kindness to my brother.

THE DRAGON'S LIES

GOD'S TRUTH

PUT ON THE ARMOR

THE MARCHING ORDERS: DAY 4

BASIC TRAINING

Ephesians 6:13-18

[13] Therefore, put on every piece of God's armor so you will be able to resist the enemy in the time of evil. Then after the battle you will still be standing firm.

[14] Stand your ground, putting on the belt of truth and the body armor of God's righteousness.

[15] For shoes, put on the peace that comes from the Good News so that you will be fully prepared.

[16] In addition to all of these, hold up the shield of faith to stop the fiery arrows of the devil.

[17] Put on salvation as your helmet, and take the sword of the Spirit, which is the word of God.

[18] Pray in the Spirit at all times and on every occasion. Stay alert and be persistent in your prayers for all believers everywhere.

DIRECTIVES

In the last chapter, you learned about our invisible enemy and how God wants you to stand firm against the strategies of the Evil One. Today, you're going to learn more about each piece of armor God has provided for you and how to use it.

Belt of Truth

Our culture wants you to believe there is no standard of truth. "You believe what you believe, and I'll believe what I believe." But God has given us his Word as the ultimate Truth.

The dragon is the father of lies, and he wants to deceive you. But Jesus says, "I am the way, the truth, and the life" (John 14:6). Whose truth will you believe? Will you believe God's Word or the dragon's lies?

Body Armor of Righteousness

Being righteous means to be full of what is right and good. But it's not just about right thinking and right acting. It's about right *being*. When you join the armies of the Dragon Slayer, Jesus gives you his own righteousness.

Philippians 3:9 says, ***"I no longer count on my own righteousness through obeying the law; rather, I become righteous through faith in Christ."***

We receive Christ's righteousness through faith!

Shoes of the Gospel of Peace

"Get your shoes on and get ready to go!" Has your mom ever said that to you?

Isaiah 52:7 says, *"How beautiful on the mountains are the feet of the messenger who brings good news, the good news of peace and salvation, the news that the God of Israel reigns!"*

When you put on the shoes of peace, you are getting ready to tell others the good news about Jesus, because he is the only one who can give you true peace.

Shield of Faith

The shield of faith will help you deflect the fiery arrows of the evil dragon. The devil will try to attack you with lies. He will tempt you to disobey God and turn away from him. But when your faith is in God, the dragon's arrows will not reach you.

Helmet of Salvation

The dragon wants you to doubt your salvation. He wants you to believe the lie that God doesn't love you or care about you. When you put on the helmet of salvation, you are protecting your mind from the lies of the dragon. You are choosing to trust in God's power to save you!

Sword of the Spirit

Did you notice that the sword of the Spirit is the only weapon God gives you to fight the dragon? All the other pieces of armor are defensive. Ephesians 6 says that the sword of the Spirit is the Word of God. How do you use God's Word to fight off the attacks of the enemy? By reading it, memorizing it, and obeying it!

Even Jesus used Scripture in a battle against the dragon. When Satan tempted Jesus in the wilderness, Jesus used passages from the Bible to fight against the enemy.

Prayer

Ephesians 6:18 tells us to pray in the Spirit on all occasions, and to stay alert and be consistent in your prayers.

Prayer is your secret weapon! You can put on all the pieces of armor through prayer. Pray the prayer below as you "put on" each piece of God's armor.

CRITICAL COMMUNICATIONS

PRAY: God of Angel Armies, I want to put on your armor so that I can stand up against the attacks of the evil dragon.

I put on the Belt of Truth. Help me identify the dragon's lies and believe in your truth.

I put on the Body Armor of Righteousness. I want to claim your righteousness as my own. Please guard my heart from evil ways of thinking or acting.

I put on the Shoes of Peace. Help me be ready to share the good news about Jesus with others. He is the only true source of peace.

I pick up the Shield of Faith. Help me trust in you. Don't let the dragon's flaming arrows near me.

I put on the Helmet of Salvation. I trust in you alone to save me. Protect my mind from the dragon's lies.

I take up the Sword of the Spirit. Give me a desire to read your Word. When I am tempted, help me remember Bible verses I have memorized.

BATTLE PLAN

On the next page, draw each piece of God's armor. Label each item and write out how you will use it.

VICTORY IN JESUS

THE MARCHING ORDERS: DAY 5

BASIC TRAINING

Romans 8:38

[38] And I am convinced that nothing can ever separate us from God's love. Neither death nor life, neither angels nor demons, neither our fears for today nor our worries about tomorrow—not even the powers of hell can separate us from God's love.

Colossians 2:13-15

[13] You were dead because of your sins and because your sinful nature was not yet cut away. Then God made you alive with Christ, for he forgave all our sins.

¹⁴ He canceled the record of the charges against us and took it away by nailing it to the cross.

¹⁵ In this way, he disarmed the spiritual rulers and authorities. He shamed them publicly by his victory over them on the cross.

Hebrews 2:14-15

¹⁴ Because God's children are human beings—made of flesh and blood—the Son also became flesh and blood. For only as a human being could he die, and only by dying could he break the power of the devil, who had the power of death.

¹⁵ Only in this way could he set free all who have lived their lives as slaves to the fear of dying.

Revelation 20:1-3, 10

¹ Then I saw an angel coming down from heaven with the key to the bottomless pit and a heavy chain in his hand.

² He seized the dragon—that old serpent, who is the devil, Satan—and bound him in chains for a thousand years.

³ The angel threw him into the bottomless pit, which he then shut and locked so Satan could not deceive the nations anymore . . . .

¹⁰ Then the devil, who had deceived them, was thrown into the fiery lake of burning sulfur, joining the beast and the false prophet. There they will be tormented day and night forever and ever.

DIRECTIVES

Courageous warrior, you have learned about your enemy, the dragon. You have learned about the pieces of armor you need to stand firm and fight against him. Keep fighting! Don't give up. Even when it feels like the enemy is winning, don't despair. He has been defeated! The Dragon Slayer has already won the war.

Go back and read each of the Bible passages in your Basic Training. Then read the corresponding messages below.

Romans 8:38 says that nothing can separate you from God's love! Not even angels or demons. Not even the powers of Hell. Not even death itself.

Be encouraged, young warrior. Jesus will fight alongside you, and he will never, ever leave your side.

Colossians 2:15 says you were dead because of your sins, but now you're alive because of Jesus! When Jesus died on the cross, he took away the punishment you deserved. And in doing so, he "disarmed the spiritual rulers and authorities." Because of Jesus, the enemy can no longer accuse you.

Hebrews 2:14-15 says that when Jesus died, he broke the power of the devil. The dragon no longer has power over you! Jesus has set you free. You don't need to be afraid of death be-cause the Dragon Slayer has conquered death.

Revelation 20:1-3, 10 gives us a picture of what will happen at the end of the world. The dragon, Satan, will be defeated! The Dragon Slayer will send an angel to bind the drag-on and throw him into a bottomless pit for a thousand years. Ultimately, the dragon will be thrown into hell and tormented for eternity.

Brave warrior, you have been given victory through the blood of Jesus. When he died on the cross, he took away the dragon's power to deceive and kill and destroy. And one day, the dragon will be destroyed forever.

CRITICAL COMMUNICATIONS

PRAY: God of Angel Armies, thank you for send-ing Jesus to die on the cross and take away the punishment I deserved because of my sin. When you died, you defeated the dragon! He no longer has power over me.

Thank you for coming back to life so I can have life as well. Help me fight bravely against the attacks of the enemy. Help me remember I don't need to be afraid of the dragon because you are always with me and you will never leave me.

BATTLE PLAN

Imagine you have a friend who is feeling discouraged and defeated by sin and temptation. How could you encourage him or her? Write a short letter to your friend on the next page. Use some of the verses from your Basic Training.

Dear Friend,
I know you've been discouraged lately.
Here's what I've been learning about
in my time with God:

Small Group Discussion

For Small Group Discussion Questions, go to

https://lauriechristine.com/dragon-slayer-bible
/discussion-guides/

THE EXTRA STUFF

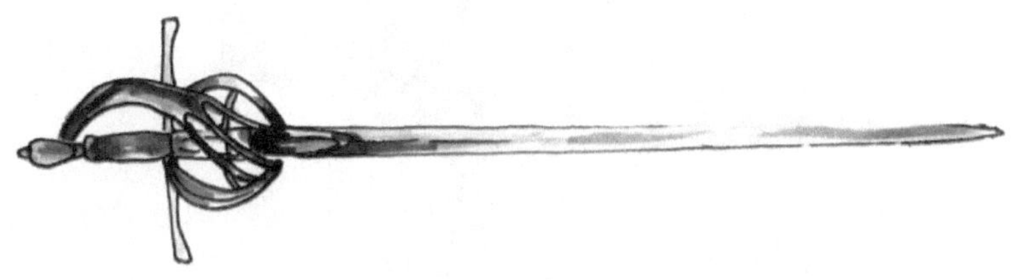

READ NEXT

THE FIRST BOOK IN
THE DRAGON SLAYER BIBLE SERIES

Garden of Mysteries

Get updates at
www.DragonSlayerBible.com

A DRAGON SLAYER BIBLE STORY
THE FIRST BOOK
GARDEN OF
MYSTERIES
LAURIE CHRISTINE

DID YOU KNOW?

God created the angels (Colossians 1:16).

One type of angel, seraphim, have six wings (Isaiah 6:2).

Another type of angel, cherubim, have four faces: an ox, a human, a lion, and an eagle (Ezekiel 10:12-14).

The angels that fell from Heaven with Satan are now called demons (Matthew 12:24).

Several angels are called by name: Gabriel and Michael (Luke 1:26-28; Revelation 12:7).

Angels are God's messengers (Luke 1:19).

Angels can't get married or have children (Matthew 22:30).

People who worship idols are actually worshipping demons (I Corinthians 10:19-20).

Jesus is much greater than the angels (Hebrews 1:1-4).

Angels are warriors (Revelation 12:7).

God sends angels to care for humans (Hebrews 1:14).

There are millions of angels (Hebrews 12:22; Revelation 5:11).

Sometimes angels appear to humans and look like humans (Hebrews 13:2).

Angels worship God in Heaven (Revelation 5:11-12).

When the Bible mentions the "angel of the Lord," it's actually talking about Jesus (Genesis 22:15-18; Exodus 3:1-5).

Angels should not be worshipped (Revelation 19:10).

BACKGROUND SCRIPTURES

Isaiah 14—Read about how Satan thought he could be greater than God.

Ezekiel 28—Read about how Lucifer became proud and rejected God.

Revelation 12—Read about the war in Heaven.

Revelation 20—Read about Lucifer being thrown into the Lake of Fire.

GLOSSARY

CHARACTERS

The Dragon Slayer—Jesus is the Dragon Slayer. He is the one God promised to send to crush the head of the dragon, Satan (Genesis 3:15).

The Dragon—Satan is the evil dragon, also known as the devil, the Serpent, and the Evil One (Revelation 12:9).

The King of Heaven / God of Angel Armies—God the Father is the King who reigns from his throne in Heaven. He is the creator of all things, and his reign is eternal (Psalm 47:8; Psalm 90:2; Psalm 93:1-2).

<u>DEFINITIONS</u>

Death—There are two kinds of death mentioned in the Bible. Physical death is when our body no longer has life. Our spirit is separated from our body. Spiritual death occurs when your soul is separated from God. The Bible says we were dead in our sins before God made us alive in Christ (Ephesians 2:4-5).

Forgiveness—When God forgives us, he promises to not count our sins against us. But God can't just overlook our sins without someone paying the penalty. Hebrews 9:22 says there is no forgiveness without the shedding of blood. But because Jesus shed his blood in our place, we can receive the forgiveness of God (Colossians 2:13-14). When we confess our sins to God, he will forgive us (I John 1:9).

God's Glory—God's glory is the total of all his attributes — his goodness, his perfection, his power, his purity, his holiness, his love, etc. When we give glory to God, it means we make his name famous. We shine a light on all his qualities so that others may see him and know him (Ephesians 3:21; II Corinthians 3:18).

Heaven—Heaven is the place where God reigns from his throne (Psalm 103:19). Those who believe in Jesus will spend all eternity with God in heaven (I Thessalonians 4:16-17). There will be no death, no sadness, and no tears in Heaven (Revelation 21:3-4).

Hell—Hell is a place of eternal torment created for Satan and his demons. It's also known as the Lake of Fire. Anyone who does not believe in Jesus and put their trust in him for salvation will also spend eternity in hell, separated from God (Luke 12:5; Revelation 20:10, 15).

Redeemer—God is the Redeemer (Isaiah 41:14). Jesus is also known as the Redeemer, sent to rescue those who have been slaves to sin and death (Galatians 4:4-5; Romans 3:23-24).

Repentance—Repentance is the act of admitting to God what you've done wrong, and then *turning away* from your sin (Acts 2:38). It's not just saying you're sorry for what you have done. You have to change the way you live (Matthew 3:8).

Righteousness—Being righteous means thinking and acting in ways that are good and pure. Because of sin, no one can be truly righteous (Romans 3:21-24). But when we put our trust in Jesus to forgive our sins, he gives us his own righteousness (II Corinthians 5:21).

Salvation—Salvation is God's plan to take care of our sin problem and fix our broken relationship with him (Colossians 2:13-14). When Jesus died on the cross, he provided the free gift of salvation. It's not something we can earn because of our good works (Ephesians 2:8-9). We receive salvation by believing in Christ's work on the cross (Romans 10:9-10).

Sin—Because of Adam and Eve's disobedience, we are all born with sin in our hearts. We also commit acts of sin. Sin is anything we do, say, think, or desire that goes against God's Word. Sin also includes things we don't do or say that we should have (Genesis 4:7; Psalm 51:5; Romans 5:12; James 4:17).

Hey Boy Moms!

I have a podcast for you!

Redeeming the Chaos is a podcast for moms who may feel a bit frazzled and overwhelmed by the responsibility of raising boys. If you want your boys to grow up to be strong, courageous young men who are fully committed to following Jesus, this show is for you. I'd love for you to join me on this wild, wonderful, chaotic adventure of raising courageous boys and connecting their hearts to Christ.

www.RedeemingtheChaos.com

FREE EBOOK

BORED WITH THE BIBLE

Do you struggle to spend time in God's Word together as a family? Is it difficult to engage your kids in family devotions?

My free ebook, *Bored With the Bible,* will help you make family devotions more engaging for your kids.

DOWNLOAD A FREE COPY:

https://lauriechristine.com/familydevotions/

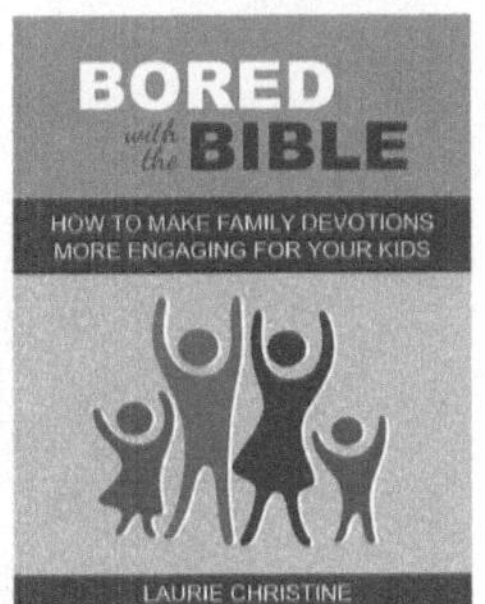

ABOUT THE AUTHOR

LAURIE CHRISTINE is an author, speaker, podcast host, Certified Biblical Parenting Coach, wife, and mom of four wild, loud, adventurous boys.

Her podcast, *Redeeming the Chaos*, invites moms of boys to join her on the wild, wonderful adventure of raising courageous boys and connecting them with Christ.

In addition to hosting a podcast, Laurie writes biblical fiction and devotions for preteen readers. Her passion is to raise strong, courageous warriors for the Kingdom of God, and to help families like yours do the same! As a mom of four boys, she understands how important it is for parents to connect with their children while communicating the truth of God's Word to them in a way they can understand.

With degrees in Creative Writing, Biblical Studies, and Education, Laurie has more than twenty years of experience in teaching the Bible to children and teens. She has also written Sunday School curriculum for her local church.

Laurie is a Certified Biblical Parenting Coach and seminar presenter for the National Center for Biblical Parenting. She teaches parents practical ways to build godly character and connect with the hearts of their children.

CONTACT LAURIE

Laurie@LaurieChristine.com

Learn more at:

www.LaurieChristine.com
www.RedeemingtheChaos.com
www.DragonSlayerBible.com

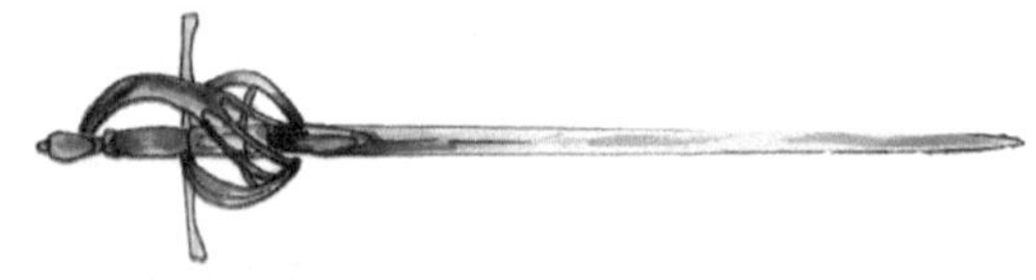

SPECIAL THANKS

My Lord & Savior—Jesus Christ;
My husband—Lynn Ressler; My sister—Lindsey
Frey; My parents—Steve & Darlene VanOrmer; My
writing critique group and cheering squad—Kelly Jo Wilson, Becca Wierwille, & Amanda
Trumpower; My business coach and marketing
guru—Thomas Umstattd Jr.

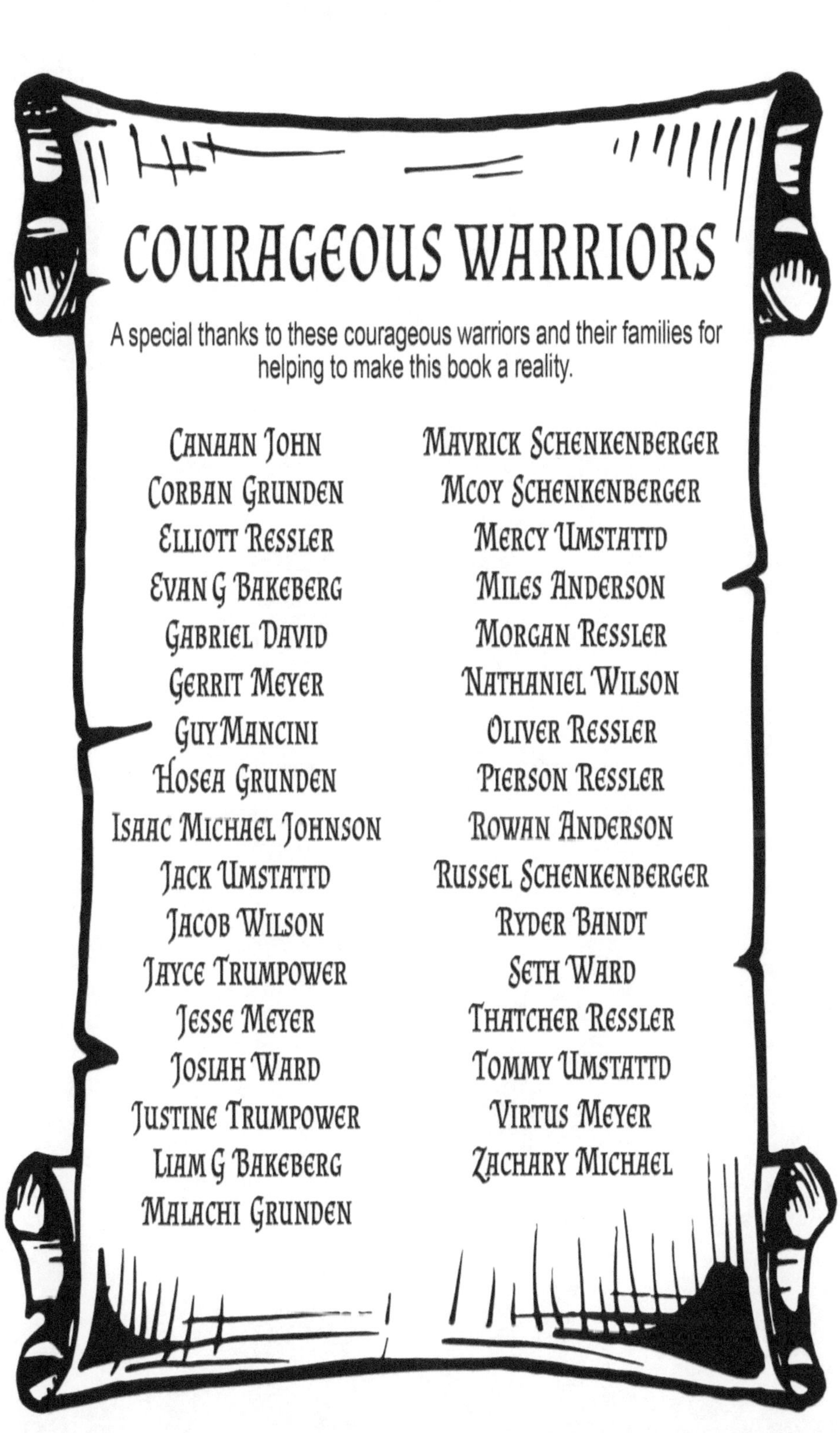

COURAGEOUS WARRIORS

A special thanks to these courageous warriors and their families for helping to make this book a reality.

Canaan John
Corban Grunden
Elliott Ressler
Evan G Bakeberg
Gabriel David
Gerrit Meyer
Guy Mancini
Hosea Grunden
Isaac Michael Johnson
Jack Umstattd
Jacob Wilson
Jayce Trumpower
Jesse Meyer
Josiah Ward
Justine Trumpower
Liam G Bakeberg
Malachi Grunden

Mavrick Schenkenberger
Mcoy Schenkenberger
Mercy Umstattd
Miles Anderson
Morgan Ressler
Nathaniel Wilson
Oliver Ressler
Pierson Ressler
Rowan Anderson
Russel Schenkenberger
Ryder Bandt
Seth Ward
Thatcher Ressler
Tommy Umstattd
Virtus Meyer
Zachary Michael